James Towne

STRUGGLE FOR SURVIVAL

WRITTEN AND ILLUSTRATED BY

Marcia Sewall

ATHENEUM BOOKS FOR YOUNG READERS

NEW YORK · LONDON · SYDNEY · TORONTO · HONG KONG

". . . and everything of worth is found full of difficulties."
~ ANAS TODKILL

Atheneum Books for Young Readers
An imprint of Simon & Schuster Children's Publishing Division
1230 Avenue of the Americas, New York, New York 10020

Book design by David Caplan
The text of this book is set in Goudy Oldstyle.
The illustrations are rendered in watercolor and sepia ink.
Printed in Hong Kong

2   4   6   8   10   9   7   5   3   1

Library of Congress Cataloging-in-Publication Data
Sewall, Marcia.
James Towne: struggle for survival/written
and illustrated by Marcia Sewall.—1st ed. p. cm.
Includes bibliographical references (p.).
Summary: Discusses the settlers of Jamestown, Virginia,
including John Smith, and the difficult early years in the colony.
ISBN 0-689-81814-9
1. Jamestown (Va.)—History—Juvenile literature. 2. Pioneers—Virginia—
Jamestown—History—Juvenile literature. 3. Pioneers—Virginia—Jamestown—
Quotations—Juvenile literature. [1. Jamestown (Va.)—History.
2. Pioneers.] I. Title. II. Title: Jamestowne. III. Title: Jamestown.
F234.J3S39 2000   975.5'4251—dc21   99-32167   CIP

FIRST
EDITION

In memory of my mother

*I*N MIDNIGHT DARKNESS, our three small ships departed Brunswick Wharf, 20 December 1606. Few noticed as the *Susan Constant, God Speed,* and *Discovery* maneuvered down the Thames River from London, sailing to the New World. We set our course for the territory of South Virginia, yet knew not what lay before us.

Troubles began just off the coast of England. Battered by contrary winds, we were forced to drop anchor. For six long weeks we waited, seasick and anxious, our supplies dwindling.

Christopher Newport, captain of the *Susan Constant* and admiral of our small fleet, discharged orders until we reached Virginia. There, the three sealed boxes with identical contents would be opened, one for each ship. Each contained the names of our leaders, chosen by the King's Council of London.

"On the 19th (20th) of December, 1606, we set saile, but by unprosperous winds, were kept six weekes in sight of England; all which time, Mr Hunt our Preacher, was so weake and sick, that few expected his recoverie."
—THOMAS STUDLEY

*M*AKING THE VOYAGE were men and four boys, together, yet not together. Of the one-hundred-and-five passengers who would settle in Virginia, over half were tuftaffety English gentlemen, unused to labor. The remainder were lower in class. I, one of the few carpenters onboard, was a Lancashire man. Going to London to find work, I found little. There was a shortage of lumber, and the city was "pestered with people." Being an unhealthy place to live, and I just eighteen, I signed on with the London Company.

Goats and hogs were in the hold of the ship, and chickens, too, all making the journey over a swallowing ocean. We were going to plant an outpost of England in the New World and raise her glorious flag on a land where the French and Spanish had already settled. We were going in search of gold and silver and riches from the Orient.

"Lastly & Chiefly the way to prosper and to Obtain Good Success is to make yourselves all of one mind for the Good of your Country & your own and to Serve & fear God the Giver of all Goodness . . ."
—INSTRUCTIONS FOR GOVERNMENT, 1606

*A*T LONG LAST WE CLEARED the coast of England. Thence, sailing southerly, we stopped at the Canary Islands to refill our casks with water. The trade winds soon carried us on to the West Indies. For nineteen days we explored those wondrous islands, ate exotic fruits and animals, and refreshed ourselves there. To our delight, Captain Newport boiled a piece of pork in bubbling hot spring water!

10 APRIL 1607: We departed and sailed northerly, following the Gulf Stream toward America. Several days past our reckoning of landfall, we sounded for the ocean's bottom, to no avail. It was suggested that we turn back, but a "cruel storm" beset us and blew us onward.

26 APRIL 1607: Four o'clock in the morning, wild shouts could be heard from the decks, "Land, ho! Virginia!"

"But, God, the guider of all good actions, forcing them by an extreme storm to hull all night, did drive them by His providence to their desired port, beyond all their expectations . . ."
—THOMAS STUDLEY

26 *April 1607:* Anchored at the mouth of Chesapeake Bay, Captain Newport took a small group of us ashore to explore. We found "faire Meaddowes and goodly tall trees." I saw much oak and walnut. But there were pine forests, too.

Lingering unwisely until dusk, we were alarmed by a handful of savages coming from the darkness. Captain Gabriel Archer was wounded in both hands and a sailor dangerously injured. Their arrows spent, we escaped.

Onboard ship that night the sealed box was opened, and the names of seven men, the Council for Virginia, were announced. Edward Maria Wingfield, Gentleman, was elected president by the new council.

In the box, too, were "Instructions given by way of Advice" for us from the King's Council in London. We were to test the high lands and hills for gold and silver, and explore the rivers for a route to the Spice Islands in the South Seas. We were to look

for the lost English colony of Roanoke. We were to settle upriver with a view to the sea and in a place where we could unload our ships with ease. We were not "to offend the naturals" but to give them our Christian religion.

29 APRIL 1607: "We set up a Crosse at Chesupioc Bay and named that place Cape Henry."

"This is all I will say to you, that suche a Baye, a Ryvar, and a Land did never the eye of mane behould . . . nowe is the kings majesty offered the most Statlye, Riche kingdom in the woorld never posseste by anye christiane prynce."

—BETWEEN *27* MAY AND *22* JUNE *1607*
UNDATED LETTER FROM WILLIAM BREWSTER

$\mathcal{F}$OR A COUPLE OF DAYS I helped assemble the shallop, carried with us from England in numbered pieces. The most of the next two weeks we explored the Powhatan River, named the James by us, and were feasted and frightened by Indians along the way.

After much deliberation we decided upon a place to settle.

13 MAY 1607: In the evening we arrived at our destination, a peninsula some forty miles up the James River with a deep channel carved against its shore. We

named our settlement James Towne (James Fort) for our king, James. Early next morning we went a-land and praised God for our safe passage.

"The thirteenth day we came to our seating place . . . where our shippes doe lie so neare the shoare that they are moored to the Trees in six fathom of water. The fourteenth day we landed all our men, which were set to worke about the fortification, and others some to watch and ward as it was convenient."

—GEORGE PERCY

*T*HAT FIRST DAY we worked hard to clear land and, finding no savages hereabouts, set up tents and lean-tos. We soon learned that we had settled on the hunting grounds of the Paspahegh Indians.

Our first night at James Towne was disturbed by savages paddling close to shore. They dispersed when alarm was given. Soon a werowance, accompanied by many men, came to visit but left, frightened by our display of gunfire. Within days more Indians arrived with an offering of venison. We suspected they came not as friends but as spies!

21 MAY 1607: Captain Newport, taking with him a party of twenty, went to explore the river. While he was away, and our guns packed in fat to keep them from rusting in this humid air, a host of Indians overcame us. A boy was killed, and most of the council injured. An arrow went through our president's beard! Though we were unprepared, shots from one of the ships' cannons put an end to the foray as quickly as it had begun.

Hastily we cut and shaped trees into a palisade to surround our settlement. With God's merciful assistance, the task was done.

". . . thus we lived near three months: our lodgings under boughs of trees, the savages being our enemies whom we neither knew nor understood: occasions I think sufficient to make men sick and die."
—CAPTAIN JOHN SMITH

*T*HE GENTLEMEN AMONG US were ignorant of work, the bricklayer wished to lay bricks, the tailor make clothes. I was happiest when using my chisel and mallet, though for several months I did little house building. Rather than be burdened with the necessary chores of farming, many refused to work at all and chose to wait for the supply ships to return with food.

In a journey to America that took five months instead of two, our food supply had dwindled, and the remaining wheat and barley "having fryed some 26 weeks in the ships hold, contained as many worms as graines."

Our leaders were quarrelsome and we were disgruntled with our lot, for we shared everything in common and there was no recompense to us for our individual labors.

The days of summer became unbearable, with no refreshing rain. We were not "seasoned to the country." Mosquitoes plagued us. There was no spring at James Towne, and slimy river water quenched not our thirst. We sickened with flux and fever.

SEPTEMBER 1607: Almost half of our colony had died, including Bartholomew Gosnold, Captain of the *God Speed.* We buried our dead in darkness.

"There were never Englishmen left in a forreigne Countrey in such miserie as wee were in this new discovered Virginia."
—GEORGE PERCY

*S*UPPLY SHIPS WERE TO BE our lifeline to England. They plied the ocean carrying more settlers, firearms and ammunition, tools, utensils, food and seed, clothing, and messages from home. And they returned to England carrying beaver and otter skins, pitch and tar, soap ash, clapboards, sassafras, and "gilded dirt," and, in time, glass, which we labored to make. Onboard, too, were homesick letters to our families.

22 JUNE 1607: Captain Newport returned to England with the *Susan Constant* arriving the end of July.

8 OCTOBER 1607: Two ships on the First Supply sailed for James Towne. *Phoenix*, separated by fog, lay over in the West Indies till early spring, arriving mid-April, carrying forty passengers. It returned to England in June.

2 JANUARY 1608: The second ship, *John and Francis*, captained by Christopher Newport, arrived in James Towne carrying eighty passengers. We were pleased to note it was "well furnished with all things could be imagined necessary." It returned to England that April.

The Second Supply of a single ship, the *Mary and Margaret*, again captained by Christopher Newport, sailed from England mid-July 1608, arriving in James Towne in September with seventy passengers. Onboard was Tom Forrest's wife and her maidservant, Anne Burras.

While the captain remained in America searching for gold and silver and a route to the South Seas, his sailors ate the desperately needed food they had brought for us. Finally, in December, they sailed home!

8 JUNE 1609: The Third Supply of nine ships sailed from England carrying six hundred passengers.

"The 22nd [June 1607] Captayne Newport returned for England for whose good passadge, and safe returne we made many prayers to our almighty God."
—E. M. WINGFIELD

OUR FIRST HOT SUMMER here was followed by a winter that turned rivers into thick ice.

7 JANUARY 1608: Worse than that, shortly after the ship *John and Francis* arrived, fire swept through our frozen village. "Many of our old men deceased, and of our new for want of lodging perished."

"Where the New Supply being lodged with the rest [had] accidentally fired the quarters, and so the Towne, which being but thatched with reeds, the fire was so fierce as it burnt their pallizadoes (though 10 or 12 yardes distant) with their armes, bedding, apparell, and much private provision. Good Mr. Hunt our preacher, lost all his library, and al that he had but the cloathes on his backe, yet [did] none ever see him repine at his losse. This hapned in the winter, in the extreame frost 1607 [–1608]."

—ANAS TODKILL (PROBABLY)

*B*UFFETED AT SEA and then on land, we were disheartened to realize our leaders' concerns were for themselves. We "were all in combustion." Membership in the Council for Virginia was forever changing, and four different men served as president in less than three years of settlement. However, during that first year, from our discordant community emerged a leader, and he a soldier, not a gentleman at that.

10 SEPTEMBER 1608: Captain John Smith was elected President of the Council for Virginia. He knew that our survival in James Towne depended on the efforts of each man. "He that will not worke shall not eate," he proclaimed, except for the sick. Displayed on a board, he recorded what each settler had accomplished in his six hours of daily work. In time, under President Smith's direction, several acres of fields were dug and planted, and James Towne doubled in size. It contented me to set to work again building houses. A guard was placed on duty day and night, and military drills were held on Saturday. Curious Indians always came to watch. The church was repaired, the old storehouse reroofed and a new one built. Boats were readied for river trade with the Indians, and a blockhouse constructed at the neck of the peninsula. I set my hand to this, too.

"[Captain Smith] who, by his own example, good words, and faire promises, set some to mow, others to binde thatch, some to build houses, others to thatch them, himselfe alwaies bearing the greatest taske for his own share . . ."
—ANAS TODKILL (PROBABLY)

*C*APTAIN SMITH, TWENTY-SIX YEARS OLD when he sailed with us, as a soldier had traveled much of Europe and farther. Until we reached the Canary Islands, when he was unjustly restrained for several months, he entertained us with tales of his adventures. And how much he looked forward to the prospects of settling Virginia!

Once here, he learned the language of the natives well enough to make shrewd deals for our desperately needed corn, often risking his life. He explored the rivers, made maps of them, and wrote about his adventures. Appointed to the first Council for Virginia, he worked tirelessly to make our new colony a success. Not always a tactful man and ofttimes a boastful one, he was both liked and disliked. But he got things done.

2 DECEMBER 1607: During the winter of the Great Frost, Captain Smith set forward in search of the source of the Chickahominy River. At the appearance of a goodly number of hostile Indians, he bound himself to his guide, but was captured, and brought before Chief Opechancanough of the Pamunkey tribe. There, Captain Smith fearlessly enchanted him with his compass. To the Indians, it was a magical thing always pointing to one star and covered with glass.

Captain Smith then told tales of the wonders of the world and of the universe. And making marks on a piece of paper (a message sent to James Towne), he proved that paper could talk!

"The King [chief] tooke great delight in understanding the manner of ships, and sayling the seas, the earth and skies, and of our God!"
                                                            —CAPTAIN JOHN SMITH

*F*ROM THENCE, IN BITTER COLD, Captain Smith was paraded from one Indian village to another, where he was entertained and feasted. He told us that he thought he was being fattened up for a meal! At last he was brought to Werowoco-moco, where the Great Powhatan, called Wahunsonacock by his people, lived. He, most powerful ruler of the tribes hereabouts, had serious questions for Captain Smith. Why had white men come to his lands? When would they leave? Captain Smith falsely assured him that our stay at James Towne would be brief, that we had been chased by Spaniards and "in extreme weather put to shore."

Later in his life he continued the story, reporting that two great stones had been placed before the Great Powhatan, and Captain Smith had been forced to put his head upon them expecting to be clubbed to death. Powhatan's daughter, Pocahontas, about thirteen years old, threw herself over Captain Smith and saved his life. Her ensuing friendship with the captain made peace, for a while, between us at James Towne, and her father's people.

2 JANUARY 1607: Four warriors returned Captain Smith to James Towne.

"After some six weeks fatting amongst those Salvage Courtiers, at the minute of my execution she hazarded the beating out of her owne braines to save mine, and not onely that, but so prevailed with her father, that I was safely conducted to James towne . . ."
—CAPTAIN JOHN SMITH

*T*HE SAVAGES TAUNTED US with tales of gold, of routes to the South Seas . . . and of corn. But we had metal tools and guns, which they desired, and pretty blue beads and tinkling bells, "which they esteemeth most." We were given by them and stolen by them, and spied upon . . . and they by us. Our ability to survive here depended on our ability to take care of ourselves, yet how many hours we wasted in search of gold. In turn, how many dangerous trips Captain Smith made up and down the river bartering for corn to keep us alive!

President Smith somehow managed to get us through a deadly winter, maneuvered us around Indian troubles, and kept the factions within our community

balanced for one brief year. Severely injured when his gunpowder pouch exploded on his lap, he was hastily deposed from office and in September 1609, Captain John Smith sailed for England never to return to Virginia.

We wondered what lay before us!

"... *for the Salvages no sooner understood of Captaine Smiths losse [departure], but they all revolted, and did murther and spoile all they could incounter.*"
—WILLIAM SIMMONS

*T*WO YEARS HAD PASSED, AND still no profit was made from our James Towne settlement. Those who had invested in the London Company's venture here were discontented. No gold filled their pockets (or ours), and our leadership was in disarray.

23 May 1609: A second charter was drawn and signed by the king. An appointed royal governor would replace our president. His instructions would come from the King's Council itself.

8 JUNE 1609: A fleet of nine ships set sail on the Third Supply under the new charter. Six hundred men, women, and children were onboard. If numbers told of success, then we would prosper. But all documents and newly appointed leaders were on one ship, the *Sea Venture*.

Beginning in August, we kept futile watch for her as others from the fleet straggled in. Four hundred needy passengers disembarked after terrible voyages, their supplies depleted. It was the beginning of the Starving Time. Hundreds tried to live on food allotted for a few. From the Indians "wee had nothing but mortal wounds with clubs and arrows." Some men turned savage and ate the dead. Like dogs, we grubbed for food, eating snakes and roots. Only sixty of us lived to see spring.

"It were too vild [vile] to say, and scarce to be beleeved, what we endured . . ."   —WILLIAM SIMMONS

*T*HE *SEA VENTURE NEVER ARRIVED.* Instead, two pinnaces, *Patience* and *Deliverance* sailed up our river, 24 May 1610, carrying 150 passengers, who, a year before, had departed from England on that ship. Caught in three days of raging tempest, when the fleet was scattered, *Sea Venture* foundered on Bermuda. Almost all passengers and crew survived there in primitive plenty. Two children were born: a boy, Bermudas Eason, and a girl, Bermuda Rolfe, and there was a marriage, too. During their stay, two smaller boats were fashioned from the one, to carry them onward to Virginia.

". . . strange it is to say how miraculously they were preserved in a leaking ship . . ." —WILLIAM SIMMONS

*E*XPECTING TO FIND a prospering James Towne, the new arrivals found, instead, what "looked lyke Anotamies Cryeing Outt we are starved. We are starved," and a food supply to last only sixteen days. The village and the palisade were in sad disrepair.

Our newly appointed governor, Lord de la Warr, unable to make the trip with the fleet, sent Sir Thomas Gates in his place. He and his assistant, Sir George Somers, saw our situation as hopeless. After repairs were made to the ships, and the remaining flour we had turned into hardtack, they ordered everyone "at the beating of the drum to repair aboard" one of the four ships tied up to shore. Confused and

exhausted, we were ready to leave our ill-fated settlement.

Food would last, we hoped, until we reached Newfoundland and English fishermen there. If luck could be with us, we would then sail homeward.

7 June 1610: Our small, woeful fleet anchored for the night below Hog Island.

"When these two Noble Knights did see our miseries . . . they embarked us with themselves, with the best meanes they could, and abandoning James Towne, set saile for England." —William Simmons

*T*HE NEXT MORNING, to our great surprise, a longboat approached us from downriver with a messenger onboard. Sir Thomas West, Lord de la Warr, our new governor, and his fleet of three well-supplied ships were not far away, the messenger shouted. Turn back! Those of us who had lived through the Starving Time turned back reluctantly. It was God's will that we had not burned James Towne in departing.

9 JUNE 1610: Our new governor and his fleet arrived carrying three hundred healthy passengers and supplies to last for a year. The following morning they came ashore to the village, and we gathered in thanks giving and to ask the Lord's blessing. Fortunately, those newly arrived were full of hope and, under new leadership, we set to work together.

With God's grace, James Towne would survive.

"Never had any people more just cause, to cast themselves at the very foot-stoole of God, and to reverence his mercie then this distressed Colonie; . . ."
—WILLIAM BOX

List of Characters

ARCHER, GABRIEL—Gentleman, original settler, appointed to the Council for Virginia.

BOX, WILLIAM—contributed to John Smith's "General Historie of Virginia."

BREWSTER (BRUSTER), WILLIAM—Gentleman, original settler, killed by Native Americans Aug. 1607.

DE LA WARR, LORD (SIR THOMAS WEST)—of nobility (related to Anne Boleyn), appointed by King James Lord Governor of South Virginia, returned ill to England after one year at James Towne, died 1618 on voyage back to James Towne.

FORREST, TOM—Gentleman.

GOSNOLD, BARTHOLOMEW, CAPTAIN—Gentleman, original settler, Captain of *God Speed*, member of first Council for Virginia, promoter, patentee, and investor in James Towne settlement. Made voyage to New England 1602.

GATES, SIR THOMAS—Original patentee of the Virginia company, sailed to South Virginia on the *Sea Venture*, appointed royal governor 1609–1610 and again 1611–1614.

NEWPORT, CHRISTOPHER, CAPTAIN—Admiral of original fleet, Captain of *Susan Constant*, appointed to first Council for Virginia, sailed supply ships.

OPECHANCANOUGH—brother of Powhatan, joint ruler of Pamunkey tribe.

PERCY, GEORGE—Gentleman, member of nobility, original settler, president of the Council for Virginia September 1609 through May 1610, writer of "Observations."

POCAHONTAS (NICKNAME), MATOAKA (PROPER NAME)—born 1595, died 1617, daughter of Powhatan (Wahunsonacock), friend of Captain John Smith, married John Rolfe April 5, 1614, son, Thomas, born 1615, sailed to England 1616, died onboard ship returning to Virginia 1617.

POWHATAN (NICKNAME), WAHUNSONACOCK (PROPER NAME)—paramount chief of the Powhatan Indians, with over thirty tribes under his control in coastal Virginia, principal residence between 1608–1609 was Werowocomoco on the York River, later moved to distance himself from the English.

SIMMONS (SIMONS, SYMONDS, SIMMONDS), THE REVEREND WILLIAM—Gentleman, editor of Captain John Smith's *A Map of Virginia*, 1612, contributed to Smith's *General Historie of Virginia*, 1624.

SMITH, CAPTAIN JOHN—born 1580, died 1631, soldier, original settler, appointed to first Council for Virginia, appointed Cape Merchant, elected president of the Council for Virginia September 1608, injured and deposed September 1609, returned to England, sailed to New England 1614 (suggested it be named "New England"), wrote of his travels and experiences. Books include *A True Relation* (1608); *A Map of Virginia* (1612); *General Historie of Virginia, New England and the Summer Isles* (1624).

SOMERS, SIR GEORGE—Admiral of the Third Supply fleet, Captain of *Sea Venture*, member of parliament, privateer, patentee of London Company, deputy to Sir Thomas Gates.

STUDLEY, THOMAS—Gentleman, original settler, first Cape Merchant, contributed writings to John Smith's *A Map of Virginia* (1612).

TODKILL, ANAS—Soldier, original settler, aide to Captain John Smith, contributed writings to *A Map of Virginia* (1612).

WEST, SIR THOMAS—(see de la Warr, Lord)

WINGFIELD, EDWARD MARIA—Gentleman, Esquire, original settler, patentee, and investor in James Towne, elected first president for the Council for Virginia April 1607, deposed September 1607.

Glossary

BARTER—fair exchange of goods between two parties

BERMUDA—largest of the Bermuda Islands

BLOCKHOUSE—a sturdy wooden fortification

CANARY ISLANDS—located off the northwestern coast of Africa

CHANNEL—deep part of a river

CHARTER—a grant from authority giving certain rights

CHESUPIOC BAY—Chesapeake Bay

CLAPBOARDS—long, narrow boards used on the outside of houses

COMPASS—an instrument used to locate directions

FATHOM—water measuring 6 feet in depth

FOUNDER—to run aground, to break apart

HARDTACK—sea biscuits made from flour and water

HOLD—below decks storage area in a ship

LANCASHIRE—a county in northwestern England

LEAN-TO—rough shelter made of branches and boughs

LONDON COMPANY—a group of London investors, promoters of the settlement of South Virginia (as it was then designated), under the authority of the Virginia Company, governed by the King's Council

MOOR—to tie up a ship

NATURALS—Native Americans

ORIENT—countries of Asia

OUTPOST—distant settlement

PALISADE; PALLIZADOES—fence made of tall, pointed wooden stakes

PINNACE—a small sailing boat

PROVIDENCE—with God's help

RECKONING—the location of a ship

ROANOKE COLONY—English colony that Sir Walter Raleigh attempted to establish on Roanoke Island, Virginia, in 1585 and 1587

SALVAGES—a spelling of savages

SASSAFRAS—bark of the sassafras tree used for medicinal purposes

SEATING PLACE—where a ship is docked

SHALLOP—an open boat with oars and sail and wooden side fins

SOAP ASH—wood ashes used for soap making

SOUND—to measure the water's depth with a weighted line

THATCH—plant stalks used for roofing

TRADE WINDS—a system of northeasterly winds in the Northern Hemisphere

TUFTAFFETY—silken dressed

VENISON—deer meat

VIRGINIA COMPANY—organized by a small group of prominent Englishmen (divided into the London Company and the Plymouth Company). On April 10, 1606, it received a charter and land grant from King James I, giving the London Company and the Plymouth Company each a limited area within a specified territory for settlement. The territory of Virginia extended from Cape Fear, North Carolina, to the Passamaquoddy River (which separates Maine from Canada) and west to the Pacific Ocean, distance unknown at the time.

WATCH AND WARD—to observe and protect

WEROWANCE—local Native American chief, could be male or female

Information Regarding The Three Ships

SUSAN CONSTANT	GOD SPEED	DISCOVERY
116' long	68' long	49' 6" long
24' 10" beam	14' 8" beam	11' 4" beam
120 tons	40 tons	20 tons
54 passengers	39 passengers	12 passengers
17 crew	13 crew	9 crew

Selected Source Material

BARBOUR, PHILIP L. (ed.), *The Jamestown Voyages Under the First Charter, 1606-1609.* 2 vols. England: Cambridge University Press, 1969.

BARBOUR, PHILIP L. *The Three Worlds of Captain John Smith.* Boston: Houghton Mifflin Co., 1964.

BILLINGS, WARREN M. *Jamestown and the Founding of a Nation.* PA: Thomas Publications.

FISHWICK, MARSHALL W. *Jamestown, First English Colony.* American Heritage Junior Library, NJ: Trull Associates, 1965.

FOSTER, GENEVIEVE. *The World of Captain John Smith, 1580-1631.* New York: Charles Scribner's Sons, 1959.

HUDSON, J. PAUL. *A Pictorial Story of Jamestown, Virginia; The Voyage and Search for a Settlement Site.* Richmond, VA: Farrett and Massie, Inc., 1957.

McCARY, BEN C. *Indians in Seventeeth-Century Virginia.* Charlottesville: The University Press of Virginia, 1957.

ROUNTREE, HELEN C. *Pocahontas's People: The Powhatan Indians of Virginia Through Four Centuries.* Norman and London: University of Oklahoma Press, 1990.

SMITH, BRADFORD. *Captain John Smith, His Life and Legend.* Philadelphia: J. B. Lippincott Co., 1953.

TYLER, LYON GARDINER (ed.), *Narratives of Early Virginia, 1606-1625.* New York: Charles Scribner's Sons, 1907.

VAUGHAN, ALDEN T. *American Genesis: Captain John Smith and the Founding of Virginia.* Boston: Little, Brown and Co., Inc., 1975.